*def*yne

poetry & writing prompts on (re)defining yourself
and defying expectations

by
douglas powell/roscoe burnems

to my children,
definitions tell us what things are.
who you are now may not be who you are later.
do not hold yourself to old definitions.

~dprb

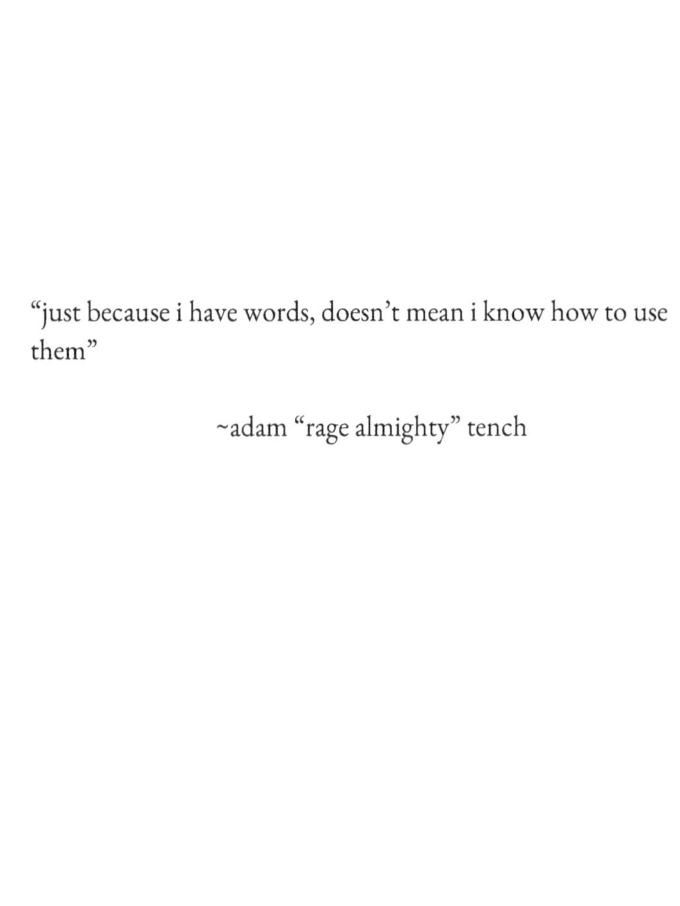

"just because i have words, doesn't mean i know how to use them"

~adam "rage almighty" tench

table of contents

def·i·ni·tion: *noun:* a statement of the exact meaning of a word (note: definition may change over time. the thing named, may name itself. it is not married to its meaning; may become something new, better, or worse)

glossary for depression
after adam 'rage almighty' tench's "*glossary*"

hard to define something when no one wants to talk about
it and when you are a black man
your thoughts on depression or therapy are two cents
that never make it to the couch cushions of a psychiatrist,
but may end with your thoughts splattered against a couch.

a friend gave me a glossary on the black man's experience.
i browsed the descriptions constantly and never found this
part of our struggle.
it sent me into a rage
so in this poem i have created a glossary:

when i say **secret**, i mean depression
feels like a child your father hid across town.
we all know it's a part of the family but we don't know
what to call it

so when i say **bastard**, i mean poor mental health.
when i say **family** i mean silence.
how no one has anything to say until you die
quietly watch you wither and then mourn the loudest

when i say **blood/y**, i mean the truth
spilling your guts feels literal
like you won't make it to the end of your confession
like you'll just be a pool of vulnerability from another black
body.

defyne

when i say **poetry**, i mean suicide attempts/notes/ideations
writing, so no one will see this as a surprise
when you finally put a period at the end of your life
sentence

lastly when i say **tree**, i mean trauma, pain
                              or problems
                              or cries for help.

as roscoe, he won championships and awards; he received
his flowers, but remained the slowest wilting rose, a petal
burning like a tire fire.
he never found the person, impersonating his impostor
syndrome. so, he was always an awkwa9*/rd smile in a room
of strangers. and by "room full of strangers" i mean: a room
with his father in it, or a room full of other people's
opinions, or a room of his own poems asking when he is
going to fully heal, or a room full of his own thoughts.

he died a martyr. he lived like one too. constantly cutting
himself open for on-lookers to grab parts they could use to
heal themselves. often when he would leave the house, he
would tell his family "if i don't make it back, avenge my
death." he got this from an episode of the simpsons.
he said it and because it was funny, but mostly because the
simpson were always predicting the future [also, how do
you seek vengeance, when the killer was his self-esteem].

roscoe was a poet's poet, a teacher's teacher, a man's man,
but never his self's self.
and died being what he loved and hated most: whatever
people needed him to be at the time.

therapy / ˈtherəpē/

noun:

1. treatment intended to ~~relieve~~ re-live or heal a disorder.
2. time travel to the worst parts of yourself to kill your insomnia.
3. butterfly effect where you step on everything.
4. realizing multiple realities are real and you decide if you want to live in the one that has all your trauma.
5. a thanos snap and you pick the parts that die.
6. the shriek when you realize you are an onion and an ogre.
7. a core: apple or earth, but you don't know if what's waiting for you is lava or seeds, but something new is bound to grow out of it. maybe you will be a tree, or...
8. an island.

after therapy

i wish i could say after every session
i rise like a resurrection.
but it's more evaporation:
a rise that changes the state i'm in

breaks me down,
builds me up,
repeat.

a cycle of pouring myself out
in drops of poetry
believing there is something valiant
in raining down.

praying i birth a garden of people
who see my mistakes and bloom better.

on social media they said lets play a game

"introduce yourself as the thing that almost killed you".

hi my name is: a car.
running into me as i was crossing the street
drive by, "duck! they shootin'!"
driving my own car off the road after i fell asleep.
driving my car off the road... on purpose.
my name is: lacking purpose and watching cars drive
by while i sit on a bridge ready to jump, wondering which car would
impale me like a knife.
my name is: knife.
knife to my gut during a fight.
knife to my neck during an argument with an ex.
knife to my own wrist.
hi my name is: suicide.
13 pills in a medicine cabinet,
[or] gasoline, lighter, and gumption.

> if i named myself after every time i tried to marry
> death,
> i'd be a multi-hyphenate of tribulation.
> but my middle name would be "but funny story,"
> and my first name is: **i'm still alive.**

here's a better game.
name yourself after all the reasons you are still alive.

hi my name is: kids
my name is: if my mother could
still find a reason to smile,
while cancers ravaged her body
(until the day she died).
then i can get my sad ass out of bed.

my name is: i tell my students to choose life,
and i can't be a hypocrite.
my name is: i still have something to say.
my voice is a victory song.
no, the pain did not make me stronger;
it showed me how strong i was already.
nights may be lonely,
but the sun will kiss me good morning.
my name is: yesterday is a memory.
my name is: god ain't done with me,
even on days when i don't believe in god

poem: *noun:* a piece of writing, speech, or song that arouses strong emotions because of its beauty; *verb:* the process of blossoming until you are plucked from this earth.

kwansaba on death and purpose

praise be to the ones before me.

that pushed my soul back into chest.

they exclaim my work was not done.

eyes awoke from my suicide attempt anew.

reeked of thanks and perfume of anguish.

i often define myself by helping others.

now i also speak to save myself.

moon pantoum

my mind becomes a galaxy
orbiting around a range of emotions.
this begats the circling of inadequacy,
still body with a mind constantly in motion

orbiting around a range of emotions.
i am a moon fighting its dark side,
still body with a mind constantly in motion
speaking sunlight and bright side.

i am a moon fighting its dark side,
wishing to be more than my clouded traces.
so i speak sunlight and bright side
to remain full, but my worth feels like it comes in phases
wishing to be more than my clouded thoughts.

i pull oceans to me to hide my tears,
to remain full, but my worth comes in phases,
and is often drowned by my fears.

i pull oceans to hide my tears,
tuck myself behind horizons and dunes
which is nearly drowned by my fears;
that's why no one knows there is water on the moon.

behind the horizons and dunes,
depression can nearly eclipse the heart,

but there is water on the moon.
and i shine because it reflects the brightest parts.

insomnia /in ˈsämnēə//

noun:

1. when your brain wakes up just late enough to wander and hate itself for it.
2. habitual and incessant falling awake, broken by moments of short-lived peace at 3 a.m.
3. the loudest form of thinking.
4. the state of being the most present when it matters the least.
5. star gazing; frantically asking the stars unanswerable questions.
6. when your self-esteem has coffee and decides to chase rabbits down a hole.
7. when your brain is all melatonin but your body is all red bull.
8. surge of electricity when a bulb wants to dim.
9. cheating on the sun with the moon.

questions i ask while spiraling mid-depression

what is death, but the last mistake you get to make?
what is a mistake, but a bad decision in an alternate reality
you regret in the now?
what is now?
what is reality, but perception?
what is perception, but an ideology you have at this
moment?
what is a "moment", but a "forever" you can't hold on to?
what is holding except the inability to let go.
what is go?
what is stop?
what is time but the way to calculate how close you are to
death?

and i think i overthink sometimes.
and the more i ask the less i know about being human.

and this is how i found god
or death
or love
or all
or none
based on the moment i'm in
but what is "in"?
intact means i'm together
interrupted means i'm apart
interrogated means i'm broken down.
intelligence means i'm building myself up.

defyne

what is "my" but possession?
when nothing belongs to us
because belong is a guarantee.
whats a " guarantee" but a sure thing in an unsure world or
an unsure maybe with too much fear to speak?
what is fear but the mind telling you?
"i know danger when i see it".
what is danger but an opportunity to live or experience
death?

what is death?
but life, after you have done.... all this dying

how are you?

and when i say i'm fine
[sometimes] what i mean is "i'm fine.
 no seriously i'm good".

[most of the time] when i say i'm fine i mean,
"your shoulder looks too sharp to lean on.
           i'm worried you'll cut me and drown me in whatever i spill
to you.

or what i really mean is "i don't trust you with all my weight;
depression can make me a lifeless body.
 this pain be a deadlift;
you can't skip leg day and expect to hold all this grief".

or what i really mean is no.
today i am swallowing hell.
my demons will stay inside, better to be a burning building than to
open my mouth and be an arsonist.
           you may enter this conversation as an empath, but you will
           leave like a burnt body after pompeii or a corpse after
           chernobyl.

most days "how are you?" is a hollow question
no one wants the depth of a real response.
no one is looking for big emotions from small talk.

or what i really mean is "you don't want to know; it's not about you!
        or you don't want to know, because it is definitely
        about you! or it's always about you and that's the problem."

or "i have always been the rock,
        the 'strong friend' you're supposed to check on, but don't
        what i have actually been is a wall with no boundaries,
        played therapist to every friend and lover
        while struggling with my own therapy sessions. and
        now, my love language is: acts of service
        while acting like i got my shit together.
        It's physical touch but emotionally unavailable".
or
         "i love you too much to let you sink in my despair.
or
        "i'm still alive and that's all i'm grateful for today.
or
        "i don't know how [or why] i'm still alive. i don't feel like
        being alive today".

and that is the scariest response
because it doesn't "validate" suicide.
doesn't help me grieve or heal.
doesn't bring my mother back.
doesn't close a casket or give closure.
it just feels exposed, dehumanizing,
or more human than i'd like to be.

what else am i supposed to say?
i'm sad? i'm anxious? i feel like i'm rotting away?
what would you do about it anyway?
since when have kind words stopped this kind of decay?

i'm   not   fine!

but i say nothing.
it feels easier to wear the mask,
and ask

25

how are you?

black /blak/

adjective:

1. complete absorption of light; harnessing everything great within.

2. rhythm put to the music of pain and triumph.

3. the sound of creativity birthed out of nothingness and became everything the world needed; the sound of influence in all american pop (see: jazz scat, boom bap, tap, bling)

4. stuck in the gray and still raising a fist against whiteness.

5. pulling resilience from a void; never avoiding who you were meant to be.

6. ageless beauty in a country that wants you to rot.

7. breathing when being suffocated by laws and lynches and laws and church fires and laws and gun smoke and laws and police brutality and laws and poverty and laws and a foot on your neck and laws and diseases-that-disproportionately-affect-you-and-people-who-look-like-you and laws and poor healthcare and...

organikkk

the sun beats down on what whiteness calls a wasteland.
steam resurrects from city streets in waves of heat.
sweat leaks from the skin, smells like soda,
or lemonade that contains no actual lemons
like water full of lead poisoning
like a flint michigan faucet
would be the perfect time though for an orange slice.
all organic cold cucumbers cut into coins.
but no one can buy that here because
ain't no whole foods in the hood

too impoverished to bite the hand that feeds them.
the people here are the first to get secondhand food boxes with ingredients
longer than the list of american atrocities.
they get meat that is met with expiration
before it meets customers.
vegetables soaked in salty cans
that used to be bullets or badges or shackles.
you can still taste the racism in these cotton-picking greens because
ain't no whole foods in the hood

the trek across a city for organic food
might as well be a sahara.
where the sun and prices rise,
but the income doesn't.

the climate here produces no fruit.
heart disease sits upon the stoop
passed down from their parents and poverty.
there is project housing where
bodies are packed like sardine cans or slave ships.
drugs are more accessible than pears or progress because
ain't no whole foods in the hood

no herbs and whole grain.
only profiling and pain.
and no hospitals close enough
to treat either one.
it's all by design.
in war, they destroy the food supply so their enemy starves.
these ain't just food deserts.
this is desert storm,
a war on health
trying to bury us in our own bodies.
but we have always been seeds.
try to turn our soil to pavement.
but that black ain't crack
unless we are a rose through the concrete.
the people here know how to grow and survive because
ain't no whole foods in the hood

black folk have yet to taste the fruit of their labor.
or fruit without pesticides, and it bugs me,

to think we were given the unhealthiest meals, but churned out the
best athletes,
given bitter fruit, but gave you the sweetest music.
they took away the brain food,
we still gave you the inventions that keep america running.
they want to take our bodies,
but give us diabetes because
aint no whole foods in the hood

they put us in food deserts and ask us how we be cactus.
how we learn to make success out of sand.
keep a fountain of youth running like a river in our bodies.
we processed the trauma and the processed food;
took your god-forsaken groceries,
and made ourselves immortal.
we had to because
ain't no whole foods in the hood.

love you 3000

i stopped arguing over who is the goat
to groups that want to herd in greatness,
but never heard you the way i did.
of course you are the greatest of all time.
but you're better than "goat ".
you are hip-hop's unicorn
whimsical anomaly, only true believers can see
appearing now only as a guest in songs
just to prove you are still real.
a black man with bars
while breaking the bars of expression and identity.

thank you andre 3000
for giving voice to black boys
who don't fit inside of the trap,
too bright colored for the block,
too nigga for a whitehouse
too eccentric for a morehouse
the unraveled artsy black boy
that can't be stitched into hoods and baggy jeans
or suit and tie,
or body bag and stereotype,
rather be turbans and wigs
camo, crochet, and kilts.

defyne

i watched my brother bark the latest dmx hits
and grit his teeth in the mirror.
i looked at my reflection and attempted to snarl,
but my reflection replied with a spottieottiedopalicious trumpet.

brothas that push cadillacs and coke
was told i was cool but i didn't fit
the puzzled existence of thugs and dealers,
and niggas who carried the weight of society in their clips anytime i
tried to skip.
dudes would detour me away from the corner:
"take your corny ass to school,
don't let me find you in these streets!
right there that's the smart nigga with the poems. he weird but he
aight tho.
i fuck with him ",
and from bass heavy chevys would drop bombs
and your verse would play;
and the same guys would say "andre?
thats that smart nigga spitting poems,
he weird but he aight tho.
i fuck with him."

and i felt seen.
i too was psychedelic prints and handmade garb.
my hair wrapped up and scribed abstractions in my notebooks.
sometimes the poems would contain the trajectory of a bullets
journey

sometimes my journey as a bullet from a cupid…
valentino or a love letter to a heartbreak,
or a broken version of me.
sometimes they would sound like hamlet
either way something would die in the end.
my stories felt extraterrestrial among humans,
and i found aliens from the planet of atlanta
and while big boi gave us the gritty rip of a staccato pimp,
you morphed into the awkward palette.
your art of storytelling made me feel
like the first frame in a gallery.

i played "elevators" when i was buried in my failures.
i played"the whole world" when i felt alone.
"roses" became the soundtrack to my divorce.
you serenaded me back to life softly
as if you played piano in the dark,
or a flute in an airport,
a pied piper to the outcasted black boys.
god emcee to the hip-hop heads without a deity.

for me you have always been the best alive,
even when you try to deny it.
but even if you aren't the one,
you are the prototype.

representation: noun: an artistic likeness or image; a
formal protest; one person standing for another so as to
have the rights of the person represented. oppressed people
seeing themselves in a world where oppression is not an
identifying term.

black dad steps up to parenthood
(after sha'condria 'icon' sibley's *"black woman steps up to mic)*

and is read as a fable

myth

black dad is a unicorn that doesn't exist they say,

but here he is

out of the shadows

of absence

black dad was a dad early

19 years old,

0 years of research material.

[this] black dad didn't have a manual for fatherhood

just a few pages of motherhood he revised to fit

learned that the instructions aren't very different.

so black dad be nurturing,

be learning and growing,

be stern and caring,

be stem and root,

be soil and sky,

be water and wind,

be what his mother would do.

black dad defines himself

by the happiness of his children;

uses their smiles as richter scale

to gauge the impact he has.

my son, the monarch

my son flutters,
floats through the kitchen,
arms out and no direction
like a butterfly playing tag with its own shadow.

this halloween a butterfly is what he asked to be unprompted.
he knows nothing of what society associates
with fancy colors and flutter;
he just loves butterflies.

do you know how hard it is to find a "boy"
butterfly costume?
there isn't one (they're all meant for girls).
they are all flowy dresses monarch gowns
fairy's turned, multi-colored insects.
but we bought one satin orange and black,
frilly bottom and wingspan bright as summer.

my son was three,
doesn't know what a dress is,
does not address it as a dress either.
only daydreams himself under the sun,
and free from his chrysalis.

in my childhood,
boys couldn't be butterflies;
boys sting
boys are wasps.
i learned to wound or to be wounded,
but never chrysalis.

chrysalis hardens but births a rainbow.
a chrysalis allows what's inside to become new.
i was taught boys don't rainbow, they scab.
scabs harden but birth a scar.
like boys can look healed but are always scarred

he was so fascinated by butterflies.
i learned things like some wings are poisonous.
ain't that a metaphor for a boy born into toxic carrying it on his
body,
on his back.
dangerous when he just wants to be beautiful,
wants to stop and smell the roses.
my son always stops mid-stride admiring a flower, sky,
or the beauty in just being alive.
he is a kaleidoscope of emotions and always breaking free
but butterflies are easy to break.
that is what scares me most
that some person will rip his angelic innocence.
i learned when a human touches a butterfly's wing,
it damages a million tiny scales.

defyne

but, if you stay perfectly still long enough,
a butterfly will rest on you.

i am trying to soften my primitive hands,
so he lives like a butterfly and doesn't die like a man.
i admire his dance in his butterfly costume
as he twirls and boasts,
plays with trucks and trains and little boy things.

sometimes he will rest his face on my palm
as if to tell me " thank you for giving me wings ".
and all this happens while i'm still in my own shell
learning from him how to be free.

firsts

as a parent, you prepare for the
first

        step
        day of school
        love.

but never the
first

        time your kid hates life,
        or
        when they want to take their own.

first
she's cracking jokes,
a desert smile, dry humor,
to evaporate the tears.
later, on the chalkboard
we use for notes and affirmations she scribbled.
      "life is rough and sometimes i hate it."
first time i caught her crying in her room,
confessing to a blade that she hated herself.
but, didn't really know why she wanted to die.
i saw myself in my daughter.
the sarcasm that could cut steel.
watching her comedian her depression away.
this was the first moment i saw the worst of me in her.

defyne

i was her age the first
time i thought of suicide and first time i attempted it.

no one tells you about these *firsts:*
time you feel like a failure as a parent.
time you don't know what to say.

first,
i wanted to show her the burns on my chest.
when i tried to make ashes of my self-esteem.
when i thought cuts turned a forearm into a map to freedom.
when i was nearly goaded by the voice
of death (or whatever speaks to you in the lonely moments)
to do a trust fall from a bridge and let an 18-wheeler catch me.
but, i feared my tales would give her ideas.

first thing i wanted to do was hold her.
drape her in that cape that every parent wears;
but, she didn't want to be held
in this tattered hand-me-down.

so we sat, in silence
a generation of depression between us
first 13 year old me, now13-year-old her.

first thing i said was:
feels like damned if you leave and hell if you stay.

sometimes the pain makes you appreciate the strength you have to
push it away.
i found love in tomorrow when i chose today.
life gives you another day to be a winner.
suicide is the last day you get to be a quitter.
i've learned so much from the attempts that withered

before i did.

my firstborn leaned in and called me a crybaby.
we laughed and talked about surviving.
she says i turn everything into a poem.

she ain't lying.

it is because i still remember the
first poems that kept me breathing.
i wrote them about her.

keloid

keloids are considered a dysfunction of a healing wound.
when the body sends more protection
to an area, it thinks is more vulnerable,
creates a memorial so the brain never forgets what happened here.

my body keeps count
of memories my mind avoids.
back, shoulders, and chest riddled with keloids
raised scars that raise so many questions,
products of the violence, the bullying, the fights, stabbings moments
when i have been a victim,
but most of the keloids i have are self-inflicted.

a killmonger chest full of death,
a tally of all the times i wanted to die
my self-esteem, the reaper with a scythe
digging into my shoulder blades,
carved into arms.
my mother's cigarettes were stolen to burn craters
just below my collarbone.

self-harm is a dysfunction of healing,
a cry for help when i needed more protection.
this is where i was most vulnerable.

picked on in school,

at home i'm being picked apart.
poverty got us picking at scraps,
anxiety got me picking at my scabs.
i cut myself open hoping to bleed out the trauma.
depression didn't just make me sad;
it made me a surgeon,
casualty of the war in my mind.
my skin tried to be a shield.
now my body looks like a battlefield of shallow graves.
it's caused me more shame than anything.
self harm ain't sexy.
interactions with women are still scary
before the inevitable reveal i would fuck with the shirt on
and the lights off;
move their hand before they slide their fingers
across the braille of my past.

my mirror still sees the boy praying for better but baptized himself
with burns and blades.
they say healing is a spiritual journey,
wished my family believed
in the highs and lows of being bipolar
as much as heaven and hell.
they said seek jesus for repair.
i see him on the cross.
jesus got keloids
from the scars on his chest,
holes in his palms.

defyne

if they won't patch up a savior,
they damn sure won't patch up a sinner.
i needed a therapist (and a doctor)
more than i needed a pastor.
they casted stones,
and the emotional scars would grow

a keloid grows to be bigger than the original wound:
the wall of a healed scar,
but ugly and unsightly
i have grown bigger than my original trauma,
but it was an ugly process that
my brain has buried in a mass grave of things i want to forget,
just to be reminded
immortalized in the gravestones engraved across my flesh.

reflection

"for as long as we live, there is always work to do"
- lenise mazyck

each session i gift my therapist all my demons.
she hangs them up for me to see
like school pictures on a fridge
to show how much i've grown
i grimace and then smile
at the old me because it is the *old* me
even if it were a me
from just a few moments ago.

mental health: *noun:* a person's condition with regard to their emotional well-being. often, in reference to a person not being well. well-meaning people will attempt to help, but the wellness of the health is dependent on the wealth of the well where the person gets their water. whether it be a wash of resilience or all tears and old wounds.

she/i
[a poem in four parts]

she [english] \ ˈshē *pronoun*

>   1.   used to refer to a woman, girl, or female

shi [japanese] \ ˈshē *noun*

>   1.   death
>   2.   the number 4
>   3.   expert, master, or teacher

shi [chinese] \ ˈshē noun

>   1.   poem

i.

the first time she died
was more metaphorical; poetic
she was buried 20 feet into depression
after my brother was sentenced to 20 years in prison.
she, felt judged as a parent and given a death sentence.
the faith she had in herself smashed under a gavel.
she refused to work, eat, or bathe,
or remember she had another son.
it took weeks of pleading, prying, and praying
til she would rise again.
if you think it's a miracle to raise the dead,
try raising a grieving mother from a bed.

ii.

the second time my mother died
was literal failure.
heart failure.
mid day before shi takes my aunt to chemo
midway through my brother's sentence,
declared lifeless on the way to the hospital.
but another emt sends one more lightning bolt
into the heart
like god striking the soil
when i got there i was shocked to see
shi was a garden; tubes sprouting like weeds
out of the mouth and nose comatosed for weeks.

doctors told me to make arrangements
instead i made a playlist of my mother's favorite gospel songs.
she rose again; a christ
a rose again, blooming once more.
this time with a battery attached to the heart
my hero, my very own ironman

iii.
the third time she died,
it was breast cancer:
same monster that killed my aunt,
same chemo that kills the soil before it restores.
rosemae, my mom,
wilted right before my eyes
shi, a victim of a war of medicines and diseases battling for space
brittling her bones,
harvesting her hair as a trophy.
life sunk from the eyes,
but shi would brag.
she still got one more fight inside.

iv.
the last time my mother died,
it felt like poetry; like the end of an epic.
all these years shi had made death wait.
her oldest son finished his odyssey
until shi could hug him as a free verse,
see him become a volta; turn his life around.
she, a rose under two suns again,
shi mastered blooming until she was done,
allowed cancer to leave the stem,
and move to the brain.
the last fight,
the endgame
the snap
the finale

i mourned my mother 4 times more than anyone should.
i learned grief is neither fair nor linear,
could never build up to *acceptance.*
step 4 never lets me live.

things they don't tell you about grief

1. denial is an understatement. no matter how long i watched my mother sink, every day i cried enough to drown an ocean, hoping she'd rise like a tide but she returned to me as sand in an hourglass. i keep turning her ashes over and over in hopes of rewinding, and nothing. they say the hands of time are always moving forward. they don't say, in grief, the hands will strangle you.

2. anger could have been the name of every stage of grief and it would have been true. i was angry in denial and angry in my acceptance. i am angry at myself for not doing enough, angry at her for not doing enough, angry at chemotherapy, angry at doctors for treating her like a game, and gave us another loss after we walked out of their practice. they say you'll be angry that she's gone. they don't tell you that you'll be furious watching other people celebrate mother's day.

3. depending on your religion, you will not do much bargaining. i will not barter with a god that let his own son die swiftly in front of him and let my mom die slowly in front of me. doesn't feel fair. my dad was a deadbeat but my mom died first. everyday i offer to trade them. okay, you may bargain a little, even if you have nothing to offer.

4. four, was the stage of cancer my mother was in when we found out. the 4th stage of grief is depression. i think depression is a cancer that was growing in my mother way before she was diagnosed. when her father disowned her, when her mother treated her like a mistake, her oldest son

was locked away for 20 years. what they don't tell you is depression is more trapdoor than a stage.

5. they say acceptance comes in the end. the catch is there is no end. grief is a jump scare on repeat. you may go months without sobbing then boo! the ghost of grief makes every name sound like your mother. it reminds me that i handed her body to a healthcare system that cared more about our insurance than ensuring she'd be okay. i have accepted that nothing guarantees that people will care about the person you cared for: not doctors, not family. they say gone too soon but do nothing to keep you here.

they don't tell you that the 5 stages are all performances in a show you never wanted to be in. in front of an audience, you don't want to show your tears to. and the reality is the show goes on until your curtain closes and you pass this song and dance on to ones who will grieve you.

death is usually defined as

the absence of life,
but i argue it is a part of life,
and it is the easiest part;
and that it is better to live and die
than to never have *lived* at all.

so, i do not live in regret
instead, i regret nothing...
live it all
write it all
because each day is a new sheet of paper i get to define.

blank /blangk/

adjective:
1. showing incomprehension or no reaction to all the feelings screaming inside you.
2. the state before "let there be".
3. everything full of nothing and the ability to be anything.
4. infant canvas; immense possibilities; nothing ruined... yet.
5. a stare; full of words but no courage to speak truth to power... yet.
6. a stare; full of words but no voice to speak truth to power... yet.
7. the ellipses right before you change your world.

*def*yne
yourself

Writing prompts for breaking free of what you have allowed to define you.

Write a poem with your name as a dictionary entry. Look up the meaning of your name and use that as the metaphor for who you are, who you were, and who you are becoming. Try this using your name as different parts of speech (your name as a noun, verb, adjective, etc.).

Define "resilience" and "adversity" using all five senses. Try to be as descriptive and personal as possible (for example: "Resilience tastes like licking the blood from my busted lip after beating my bully." Or "Adversity sounds like fists pounding against steel doors, fast as a beating heart.")

douglas powell/roscoe burnems

defyne

The pantoum is a poem of any length, consisting of four-line stanzas. The second and fourth lines of each stanza serve as the first and third lines of the next stanza. The last line of a pantoum is sometimes the same as the first.

Write a pantoum comparing yourself to something that rises and falls (yo-yo, sun, tide, etc.). Juxtapose the object's movement with your trials and tribulations and what you have overcome.

A kwansaba is a poem of praise. It is a seven-line poem that consists of seven words in each line. The words in each line cannot have more than seven letters.

Write a poem praising yourself for what you have achieved or overcome, or write a kwansaba about a person who has had a major positive impact on you.

Use a moment that was a turning point in your life. If this moment is a tragic one then use this poem to redefine the moment and talk about something you learned from this. Use as many similes as possible to create imagery. Be descriptive, and appealing to all the senses.

On a separate sheet of paper, perform a "stream of consciousness":
set a timer for 3 minutes and begin writing without stopping or
editing. At the end of your freewrite, using a highlighter, mark
words and phrases that stand out. take one of the highlighted lines or
words and use that as the title or first line of the poem. begin your
poem centered around the idea or premise of that line. unpack it
completely in a free verse poem.

douglas powell/roscoe burnems

66

defyne

9 798890 902603